Ulma and Upton

Pam Scheunemann

Consulting Editor, Diane Craig, M.A./Reading Specialist

Published by ABDO Publishing Company, 4940 Viking Drive, Edina, Minnesota 55435.

Printed in the United States.

Credits
Edited by: Pam Price
Curriculum Coordinator: Nancy Tuminelly
Cover and Interior Design and Production: Mighty Media
Child Photography: Steven Wewerka, Wewerka Photography
Photo Credits: AbleStock, Comstock, Anders Hanson, Photodisc

Library of Congress Cataloging-in-Publication Data

Scheunemann, Pam, 1955-
Ulma and Upton / Pam Scheunemann.
p. cm. -- (First sounds)
Includes index.
ISBN 1-59679-202-7 (hardcover)
ISBN 1-59679-203-5 (paperback)
1. English language--Vowels--Juvenile literature. I. Title. II. Series.

PE1157.S335 2005
428.1'3--dc22

2004059225

SandCastle™ books are created by a professional team of educators, reading specialists, and content developers around five essential components that include phonemic awareness, phonics, vocabulary, text comprehension, and fluency. All books are written, reviewed, and leveled for guided reading, early intervention reading, and Accelerated Reader® programs and designed for use in shared, guided, and independent reading and writing activities to support a balanced approach to literacy instruction.

Let Us Know

After reading the book, SandCastle would like you to tell us your stories about reading. What is your favorite page? Was there something hard that you needed help with? Share the ups and downs of learning to read. We want to hear from you! To get posted on the ABDO Publishing Company Web site, send us e-mail at:

sandcastle@abdopub.com

SandCastle Level: Beginning

Uu

ABCDEFGH
IJKLMNOPQ
RSTUVWXYZ

abcdefgh
ijklmnopq
rstuvwxyz

Ulma

Upton

umbrella

underwear

umpire

unzip

unhappy

Here is the .

The long is red.

Here is the .

Bill can [zipper picture] his coat.

Joe is very .

Ulma is under the umbrella.

Upton is unhappy.

Upton is happy under Ulma's umbrella.

Which of these pictures begin with u?

More words that begin with u

uncle

under

unfit

until

up

uphill

upon

us

About SandCastle™

A professional team of educators, reading specialists, and content developers created the SandCastle™ series to support young readers as they develop reading skills and strategies and increase their general knowledge. The SandCastle™ series has four levels that correspond to early literacy development in young children. The levels are provided to help teachers and parents select the appropriate books for young readers.

Emerging Readers
(no flags)

Beginning Readers
(1 flag)

Transitional Readers
(2 flags)

Fluent Readers
(3 flags)

These levels are meant only as a guide. All levels are subject to change.

Play Time

Let's Play Tug-of-War

By Sarah Hughes

Children's Press
A Division of Grolier Publishing
New York / London / Hong Kong / Sydney
Danbury, Connecticut

Photo Credits: Cover and all photos by Maura Boruchow
Contributing Editor: Mark Beyer
Book Design: Michael DeLisio

Visit Children's Press on the Internet at:
http://publishing.grolier.com

Library of Congress Cataloging-in-Publication Data

Hughes, Sarah, 1964-
Let's play tug-of-war / by Sarah Hughes.
p. cm. – (Play time)
Includes bibliographical references and index.
Summary: A group of children play a game of tug-of-war and explain the rules.
ISBN 0-516-23115-4 (lib. bdg.) – ISBN 0-516-23040-9 (pbk.)
1. Tug of war (Game)—Juvenile literature. [1. Tug of war (Game)] I. Title.

GV1098.H84 2000
796.2—dc21

00-025908

Printed in the United States of America.
1 2 3 4 5 6 7 8 9 10 R 05 04 03 02 01 00

Contents

My name is Tim.

Look at the **rope** that I found in my **garage**.

I can use it to play **tug-of-war** with my friends.

ZONE
THE COMPETITOR
REQUIRED
Lite
5

Bill, John, and Frank are my friends.

We have to make sure the rope won't break.

We pull on it to see if it will break.

We pull very hard on the rope.

It doesn't break.

It is a good rope to use for tug-of-war.

We take the rope to the park to play.

The park has grass that is soft.

If we fall on the ground, we won't get hurt.

21

We make two **teams**.

John is on my team.

We will play against Bill and Frank.

We tie some cloth in the **middle** of the rope.

We put two sticks in the ground.

The sticks are far apart.

21

We start with the cloth in the middle of the sticks.

To win, one team has to tug the cloth past the stick.

Ready, set, go!

Pull! Pull! Pull!

Tug! Tug! Tug!

John and I are not strong enough.

Bill and Frank tug the cloth past the stick.

They win!

New Words

garage (guh-**roj**) a place to park cars or store things

middle (**mid**-el) the part that is the same distance from each end

rope (**rohp**) thick string

teams (**teemz**) groups of two or more people who play a game together

tug-of-war (**tug uv wor**) a game where two teams pull a rope past a spot to win

To Find Out More

Book
The Big Book of Games
by Dorothy M. Stott
Dutton Books

Web Sites
Games Kids Play
http://www.gameskidsplay.net
This site has a list of many games that kids can play. There are rules for each game.

Richardson School—Best Games in a Small World
http://www.richardsonps.act.edu.au
At this site, you can learn new games to play. It gives the rules for each game.

Index

About the Author

Sarah Hughes is from New York City and taught school for twelve years. She is now writing and editing children's books. In her free time she enjoys running and riding her bike.

Reading Consultants

Kris Flynn, Coordinator, Small School District Literacy, The San Diego County Office of Education

Shelly Forys, Certified Reading Recovery Specialist, W.J. Zahnow Elementary School, Waterloo, IL

Peggy McNamara, Professor, Bank Street College of Education, Reading and Literacy Program